SUPERHEROES WEAR MASKS

MW01154376

CHRIS STEAD

SUPERHEROES WEAR MASKS

Text and Images Copyright © 2020 Old Mate Media

All rights reserved.

No text or images may be reproduced wholly or in part in any form of media without prior written permission from the creator, Chris Stead, of Old Mate Media.

The characters, setting and story are fictional and were created in full by Chris Stead, owner of Old Mate Media. The entire contents of this book are the copyright of Old Mate Media. This is a fictional work.

Story by: Chris Stead
Design and Editing by: Chris Stead
Illustrations by: Yohan Priyankara
Producer: Kate Stead
Published by: Old Mate Media

For more info, please visit:
www.oldmatemedia.com

ISBN Paperback: 978-1-925638-83-7
ISBN Hardcover: 978-1-925638-84-4
ISBN Digital: 978-1-925638-85-1

DEDICATED TO

All those individuals that have chosen to be brave,
in all its many facets, during this pandemic.

GET YOUR QUARANTINE
HOME ACTIVITIES BOOK

Scan this QR code to download the first
day of our Ultimate Isolation Activities
Guide for Kids **FOR FREE!** It's an
essential survival kit for parents.

MASKS are SCARY, aren't they?

Mummy and Daddy want me to wear
a MASK sometimes.

But I don't want to.

I just don't like MASKS very much.

They make it hard to tell who my mum is and who is my dad

I can't see if people are HAPPY or SAD or ANGRY.

And MASKS sure are uncomfortable to wear.

They make it feel funny to breathe and the straps always rub on my ears.

One day Mum and I had a big **FIGHT** over
wearing a MASK.

I got sent to my room to "think about it."

So, I started to draw pictures of all the people
I know who wear MASKS.

Why do they do it? Do I really need
to be SCARED?

Like Dave the builder, who came to build a new room at our house.

It was so COOL when he let me hold the hammer and hit a nail.

And I LOVE to measure distances with his measuring tape.

Dave always had the biggest SMILE on his face and told very funny jokes.

But when he was using the big saw, he always wore a MASK.

He didn't want any of the sawdust to get into his nose or his mouth.

If he breathed it in, the dust would get in his lungs and make him SICK.

I don't want Dave the builder to get sick.

Or my mum's friend Lynne; she's a doctor.

She is always so KIND when I'm feeling sick or have HURT myself.

She's very gentle when she's putting on creams and bandages.

And sometimes she even gives me a lollipop.

YUMMY!

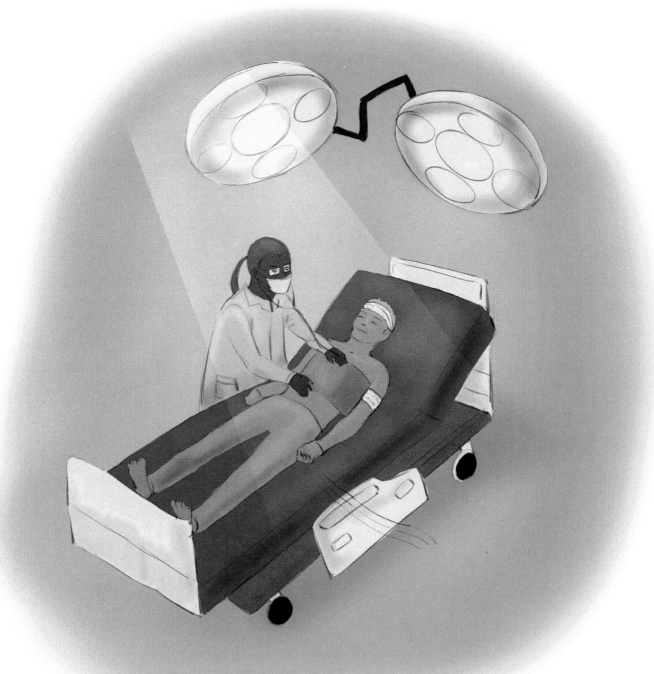

When I went to visit her at the hospital
she wore a MASK.

She has to be very CAREFUL when she
is helping people who aren't well.

If any germs float through the air and get into
her lungs she will get sick.

I don't want Lynne the doctor to get sick.

Every time I hear a siren, I think
of James the fireman.

His job is so COOL, but it's also kind
of HOT, too.

He always comes to our house with armfuls
of wood to put in our firepit.

Then we roast marshmallows and sing songs.

When he's off fighting fires, though, he always wears a MASK.

Even as he holds a hose in his hands blasting water at wave after wave of flames.

It's so the smoke from the burning trees doesn't get in his lungs as that would hurt him BADLY.

I don't want James the fireman to get sick!

Some of my favourite playtimes have been with my friend's mum, Megan.

She's a chemist and knows all these AMAZING tricks for making strange mixtures.

It's so much FUN watching her turn solids into liquids.

Or making things change COLOURS in weird and wonderful ways.

When she's in the laboratory making new products, she wears a MASK.

Some of the chemicals she mixes can release a POISONOUS gas.

If it wafts up into her nose it could get into her body and she might DIE.

I don't want Megan the chemist to get sick!

Just last week I saw my friend's big brother Mark at the park.

He has always been very GENEROUS and friendly to all the little kids.

Mark works at the fruit shop and gives me a FREE apple when we do our shopping.

He can push the swing higher and faster than anyone else I know. too.

I hadn't noticed before, but he wears
a MASK at work.

When we buy our food, I know he is SMILING
even though I can't see it.

But he sees so many people every day he must be
extra CAREFUL.

I don't want Mark the fruiterer to get sick.

Come to think of it, I don't want anybody I know
to get sick.

Especially Nanna and Pop, who are the best at
CUDDLES and reading me books!

So, if all these nice people I know wear MASKS
every day at work...

Maybe MASKS aren't that SCARY after all?

I wish I didn't have to wear a MASK.

They're still UNCOMFORTABLE and they
don't make me look cool.

But when you think about it, the people behind
the MASK aren't scary.

They just don't want to get sick. And perhaps
I don't want to either. After all...

SUPERHEROES
WEAR MASKS!

ULTIMATE AT HOME
ACTIVITIES FOR KIDS

150+ FUN GAMES

KATE & CHRIS STEAD

THE ESSENTIAL PARENT'S SURVIVAL KIT FOR COVID

14 themed days of step-by-step instructions that grant you access to over 150 free activities. Your kids will love it! Go to...

geni.us/activitiesguideA

DISCOVER MORE BOOKS BY CHRIS STEAD

THE WILD IMAGINATION OF WILLY NILLY SERIES

HELP YOUR KIDS TALK THROUGH THEIR ANGER AND FEARS

Help your child conquer depression and the many demons that make them feel sad, frustrated and angry. Very useful during COVID. Go to...

geni.us/LTSTOAmazon

AND MANY MORE TITLES – VISIT OLDMATEMEDIA.COM

Made in the USA
Las Vegas, NV
19 August 2021

28441591R00021